The Choreography of Nests

Ingrid Keir

 FEATHER PRESS

Published by Feather Press | featherpressbooks.wordpress.com

Second Edition, 2024. First published in 2016.
Printed in the United States of America

Copyright © 2016, 2024 by Ingrid Keir
Drawings copyright © 2016 by Kelly Ording

All rights reserved. No part of this publication may
be reproduced without the express written permission
of the author.

For information about permission to reproduce selections
from this book, please contact: featherpressinfo@gmail.com

Cover design by Jennifer Barone | jennbarone.com
Cover art by Kelly Ording | kellyording.com

Author contact: Ingrid Keir: ingridkeir@me.com

—

Library of Congress Cataloging-in-Publication Data

Keir, Ingrid
The Choreography of Nests : poems / Ingrid Keir
1. Keir, Ingrid II. Title

ISBN-10: 0-9979362-0-7
ISBN-13: 978-0-9979362-0-9

For Sierra
My favorite living room dance partner

I am the poet of the body,
And I am the poet of the soul.

The pleasures of heaven are with me,
and the pains of hell are with me,
The first I graft and increase upon myself…
the latter I translate into a new tongue.

— Walt Whitman, "Song of Myself"

Table of Contents

One

Remembrance	1
Dear New Year	3
Dear You	4
Dear You	5
Betrayal	6
Closed	7
Potential Book Titles	8
Dear You	9
Dear You	11
Dear You	12
Dear You	13
Dear You	14
Dear You	15
Colors	16
Absence	17

Two

Dear Summer	23
Dear Weatherman	24
Dear Winter	25
Dear Reader	26
Psalm	27
Dear Erica Jong	28

Dear Journal	29
Dear Sierra	30
I Meant To Say	31
Courage Is	32
Dear Winter	33
News	34
Dear N+7+8	35
Riddle	36
Dear Reader	37
Dear Reader	38

Three

Dear Loneliness	44
Dear Love	45
Crave	46
Drought	47
You	48
Enough	49
Dear Bravery	50
Dear You	51
Strength	52
To My Mother-In-Law On Blocking Her From Social Media	53
Dear Hope	54
Dear Love	55
Encounter	56
Dear Love	57
Desire	59
Dear You	60
Definition	61

Dance me to the children who are asking to be born
Dance me through the curtains that our kisses have outworn
Raise a tent of shelter now, though every thread is torn
Dance me to the end of love

— Leonard Cohen

...There are places on the planet
where once you did some thing so extraordinary everything
was altered. The very ground, intersection
of air and earth, longitude and latitude,
manzanita and dune, owl, ocean, redwood and asphalt altered.

— Sharon Doubiago, "The Geography of My Soul, 2"

Remembrance

⟵—————————————————————⟶

By sorrow, that runs along roads and sidewalks, dusty paths,
as we shed our lives, our skin, to become something raw.

By legs, which carry the weight of it all, past the mallards
and redwoods that sit in meditation.

By a bedfellow named sadness, shorn, weathered, and hit
by rumbling waves, ground down to humble sea glass.

By a heart and a mind, how these two constantly interrupt
one another even though of the same body.

By grief, that is not linear, but diagonal, circular,
hexagonal, triangular. The prism follows early in the
breath of new sunlight.

By a lush garden, magenta dahlia blooms, by prayer that
    become the days released with the puff of a dandelion.

By anger, oh ebony of night, the stench of thick tar spread
    on the neighbor's holey roof.

By trust, once an impenetrable hardwood, burnt to ash
    and spread in the Tyrrhenian Sea.

By shock, a swift electric current, that absorbs the brunt
    of inertia, day after day.

By acceptance, to cherish the sea glass, a relic you settle
    into as light and fire and bodiless spirit.

Dear New Year,

At the knife's edge. Await the embargoed heart. The year on which I totter will change me into a reptile. Incapable of warming without the sun. Once, we spoke the same dialect. Now we interact as if no language could connect us. A world too full of crags and cactus. I obsess over the terrain of my countertops. Garage clutter, the remnants of you, memory pulses within the cardboard box of Christmas lights. Perhaps we are avian. Crows. We migrate to and from one another; we cackle and chirp. No nest to share. It has been swept away by the storm. Neruda whispers *If suddenly / you forget me / do not look for me, / for I shall already have forgotten you*. Time to cross.

Dear You,

Head above the surface. Words shimmer: co-parenting, positive, third-hand smoke. Legalese surrounds and abounds. I am here to finish. Drive the stake in. Eternal. To mother. As in mothering. A voice arises from the depths. The dings of a mobile phone signify. Only one crow. He wiggles back-and-forth on a branch as if in a rocking chair. Morning orders. My cat creeps along the fence. This day starts with the reverence of a parade.

Dear You,

What I want to know, is how it feels to be severed. We breathe on, the questions linger like the soft crawl of the moon across the bay. Where has this new life taken you, how does it bode? Separated by time, not enough, and space ever widening. What I want to know is if she kisses you the way I once did, if she is ever going to be enough, I want to let you travel through my body, a shadow of history. The darkness and then light. I don't want to know what flowers she likes; I want to exist in the murkiness of unknown. Don't tell. Don't ask. *The temp* as our friend calls her. Puzzling, slightly off color, faded, worn.

Betrayal

←――――――――――――――――――――――→

Needles in eyes. Thick spotted black mold. Silence. A relentless sea. Unanswered questions, unseen consequences. Her face in my neighborhood restaurant, haggard and plain. To negate a vow. It lurks in shadows, an electric eel. Burn everything that meant anything. Close your eyes and run headlong into traffic. Fingers crossed behind your back.

Closed

←——————————————————→

Come again. Encinal Market on Sunday at ten o'clock. The Sesshu Foster book lying on the nightstand, the chapter of my thirties. The airplane door, the seatbelt, water bottle in hand, there for soul's dehydration. YMCA. Plastic shower curtain. Terrycloth robe, slippers, Levi's. Leather boots, front door, car window. Preschool, café, courthouse. A heart. A fist. Eyes. Sunset.

Potential Book Titles

←—————————————————————————→

Cowards Are Us
You Don't Deserve Context
Ethical Slut
Cryptic Messages
Radical Honesty
Release the Kraken
The Divorce Diet
Getting to Apathy
Phantom Limb
Impulse Control
Love's Shadow
Advice for the Weary
Twenty-Four Moons
Epistolary Convoys
Enough
The Choreography of Need
The Choreography of Crows
Impermanence
Crow's Nest
The Art of Longing
Letters I Can Never Send You

I want to know what you have inside you. I want to see the contours of your second beating heart. So write....Not like a girl. Not like a boy. Write like a motherfucker.

— Sugar, *Tiny Beautiful Things*

Dear You,

There are different stages to getting over you. The rage-rage-against-the-dying-of-the-light-Dylan-Thomas stage. The try-quickly-to-replace-you-with-another-partner stage. The go-out-and-shag-whoever-you like stage. A nice distraction, but overall takes more energy than I have time. The oh-I-think-I'm-over-it-but-just-saw-a-ghost-I-thought-was-your-girlfriend-NOT-OVER-IT stage. Setback to crying-on-the-sidewalk-stage. The half-marathon-running-stage where I conquer both my body and mind. The I'm-feeling-good-but-then-you-come-over-and-give-me-that-sad-eyed-look stage. The crying-in-the-car stage, which stopped for a while but comes and goes as it pleases similar to a FELINE. The social-media-overload stage, where being connected digitally is the sad antidote to loneliness. The staring-fear-in-the-face-stage, where moving onward is not my choice, but I must go. The unfriending stage, where you want in, but I refuse. The cougar-stage where young men are entertaining and varied. The dump-everyone stage where I realize being with myself is better company. The only-have-time-for-friends stage. The nonsensical-dream stage where I think you'll come back. The focus-on-the-bright-light-of-your-DAUGHTER stage, which is not really a stage but a fierce dedication. The BAM-out-of-nowhere stage, where I am hit with an unexpected wave of misery and how our love went off the rails. The write-write-write-like-a-motherfucker stage where I realize a U-Turn can provide perspective. The mourning-you stage, how to function without the limb on which I used to lean.

Dear You,

There are things I miss. The heated teacups before pouring in the liquid. How you gave away money to panhandlers. Something about this act was so tender and open. *There is no right way to live your life.* Wolf-blue eyes, guilt afloat. Silver threads, a torn web. Not my job to put you at ease. I weave threads nightly, try to repair. We do not speak of it. Cowardice. Calm horror of silence. Swift gallop of departure. The border is scorched. Wall thick as steel.

Dear You,

The terrain of emotional purgatory. Cactus and red rock. *I love you. When you're not happy I'm not happy. I'm sorry for all this.* Sleepless. A process of hold. Rigorous anguish. When the command of language fails, respond with Adrienne Rich. *From you I want more than I've ever asked, / all of it—the newscasts terrible stories / of life in my time, the knowing it's worse than that, / much worse—the knowing what it means to be lied to.* I am a soul in the Mojave. I lie down, the Red-tailed Hawk spirals. To be sucked dry; marrow fed on by vampires and Yucca. A woman who has crossed over, sandbags dropped in the canyon.

Sometimes the body
Gets so quiet
it can hear the soul
scratching like something trapped
inside the walls
and trying frantically
to get out

— Kim Addonizio, "Body and Soul"

Dear You,

Apple blossoms. Tethered to blue-black wings, I flap and struggle under my own weight. I am an unsigned participant, the lone figure throwing out peanuts and mismatched socks. Moored to dahlias, castor beans, ferns. The ropes are translucent quartz. The psychic desire to undo, but we've been bound by centuries. I do not understand the riddle until she looks into her crystal ball. She sees our souls have been caught in this web for lifetimes. A curl of grey hair in a heart-shaped locket. A box of matches from Paris. I bury these relics by the sea. The crows watch all of this from their perch.

Dear You,

In Linda's one-room cabin in Mendocino, I awoke from sudden sharp pain. I dreamt of a splinter wedged under my fingernail. The smell of redwood, walls surrounded by low light. Green furry trunks loom. Shadows as warmth. Miniature wood fired stove. My hand transformed to paw. I am spotted leopard with patterns of persistence. I tread the underbrush and forest floor.

Dear You,

This storm kicked off the power for thousands of people. Four to five inches of wet. When the garage started to flood I realized that's when I missed you. To handle floods and hairy spiders. *Are you alright?* Scent of earth and loam. Is that a rhetorical question? I say *yes*. Leave it. I try to steer the course with minimal disruption. Rosewood beads. The heavens throw down a river of surrender. Universal truth. Neruda.

During the blue nights you think the end of day will never come.

— Joan Didion, *Blue Nights*

Colors

←——————————————————————→

Not purple but grey. Not black but the matte shadows of a trash bag. Not crimson, not desolate, not awake. Not twenty-nine, not thirty-nine, but forty. Not old aged but middle aged. Not eight hours of sleep but six. Not a week but a weekday. Not deliberate but a reckless blow of Maceo's horn. Not Sunday but Monday. Not face-to-face but digital. Not spoken but understood. Not safe for work. Not grey but heather grey. Not juicy but dehydrated. Not together but apart. Not separate but separated. Not married but mourning. Not equal but justice. Not clear but cloudy. Not royal but endless sapphire.

Not the tinge of memory in a place where someone else stood unaware of your life or its constant necessity to record its existence in each room's sharp corner

— Maxine Chernoff, "Rune"

Absence

←——————————————————→

Not the Sunday dinners prepared with garlic that lingers on fingers the next day, a reminder of a lengthy and intricate recipe.

Not the *New York Times* read leisurely in the morning as printed black ink rubs onto hands and fingers; section upon section discarded to the floor like a manuscript of the world in the fold.

Not the weekly trip to the farmer's market where the children play in the manmade stream under the Eucalyptus trees and yellow bulbous sun.

Not the taste of *PG Tips* with honey and milk as a daily morning ritual.

Not the sound of a diesel engine purring in the driveway at 6:02 p.m.

Not the vows we promised in front of our tribe, which now ring in silence.

Not the touch of your hands on my body in the night.

Not the smell of sweat in a beard that should be washed and trimmed and begins to mimic the likeness of a Muppet.

Not the light in the garage as you shut out the world to draw lines on stark, blank paper.

Not the truth of your departure, a ring of circles that widen and widen.

Not the laughter forfeited, gone with the migrating humming birds.

Not the weekend getaways to the foggy coast where we would sleep in the back of a truck, days spent in healing hot water.

Not the choreography of need, but the pirouette of an aria as feathers float toward her window at sunrise.

Not the icy stalactite that melts away to nothing but a ripple in a puddle of evaporated water.

...if we are willing to tolerate our crow-related uneasiness and accept certain lessons, there is hope....Hope that we can learn another kind of attention that is deeper, wilder, more creative, more native, more difficult and far more beautiful.

— Lyanda Lynn Haupt, *Crow Planet: Essential Wisdom from the Urban Wilderness*

Dear Summer,

Love is diagonal, not unlike the whir of a machine, buzz of an insect, mad dash of Canadian geese in the running bath. I step off the curb, fifteen seconds later, two cars crumple like used Kleenex, my legs free to continue walking down the street as sirens flood the night's quiet. When two people, traveling on varied paths directly miss one another, is it an omen of good luck or bad? The soccer player kicks the ball to bend into the net, the way light bends into a rainbow's curve. He gazes across a crowded bar as if only I exist. I recall my first softball glove, how unexpectedly delicious the leather hide smelled of something nearly briny, yet not of the sea. The giant ball lands directly in my palm, but love is not something to be caught. Minutes tick away. A letter arrives and proclaims to be love or lost love or who the hell knows. We write to one another about mystery and longing and ghostly characters who survive sweaty summers on NYC asphalt. Condensed sweat drips from air conditioners, a rain of rapture down from concrete heavens. Machines purr in the bedrooms of lonely women and pull out orgasms like hot pasta: wet, steamy, noodles.

Dear Weatherman,

Could I name the color of wind cobalt? The dance of the tree bends to words like *pliable* and *arc*. Tell me of curves. Tell me the things no one else dares. Only five crows today, the storm coined "a river in the sky." Talk about revelry on the weather channel. Delirium of rain slicker hypothesis. I want my crows back. *Come again another day.*

Dear Winter,

Gentle fog. My daughter's smile. Tap of the drum. Lull of the flute. Sade's croons wash over me, a bath. Chamomile. How to inhabit? How to see duality, both flex and stretch. How to be around people and feel such solitude. I slither away. I've scraped the bottom. And what floats to the top? Lichen. Ocher. Cotton. Rock.

Dear Reader,

This poem asks you to be still. What is the texture of stillness? Notice the reward of silence, purgatory of comparison, the long day's journey, the body bolts from one place to another, a rush of hyperbole. This poem stands in solidarity for the hustle, the labyrinth of loops and curves, the never-ending parade. Sound travels far and fast. This is my prayer, my megaphone.

Psalm

⟵—————————————————⟶

Forest of dusty pine
ancient with desire,
earth's floor
held together by
needles and the scent of hope.
This is not time
to mourn inertia.
Eyes grasp blossoms,
flashes of yellow medallions
sprinkled on the hillside.
The clouds puff,
urge you to move.
Optimism rains
on everything beneath,
a baptismal.
All you long for
is already
in great supply.

There is pain enough to nourish us everywhere; it is joy that is scarce.

— Erica Jong, "Testament (Or, Homage to Walt Whitman)"

Dear Erica Jong,

You have kissed the lips of cherries and paraded in Neruda's leaves, tell me what to do with such darkness. I scribble on stark sheets, sip sweet black tea with honey and milk, fly to foreign lands, but sorrow is a boulder in my carry-on. It cannot be forever that this weight anchors me to the bottom of the ocean. Eros is burnt. The seven-year-itch mythology, realized. I have descended into the ninth circle of Dante's *Inferno*. My name tattooed on his flesh, an ancient chant. Betrayal sticks to skin. Grit creates pearls. No paper can contain me, a loose-lipped leopard pacing just outside the fence. Fearless Poet of Flight, please answer my feeble request for counsel.

My memories are stained with the familiar.
They are not perfumed with silence.

   — Justin Chin, "Imagining America"

Dear Journal,

Kernel of remembrance, list of desires, chatter of a crowded mind, move cobwebs aside, push past the critics. Excavate details. Fruit flies in an empty kitchen, the house hushed without a toddler. I miss her high-pitched squeal as she squishes my face and hollers *"TEEKLE TEEKLE TEEKLE"* while tickling my neck. The bowl of memory, she splays herself on the dirty kitchen floor and yells *"MAMA LOOK I AN OCTOPUS!"* I arrive here in the morning to scribble, to note the calamity of crows in the adjacent yard. I serve morsels of language, recite the swirls of black ink, records of recollection.

All days are nights to see till I see thee,
And nights bright days when dreams do show thee me.

— William Shakespeare, "Sonnet 43"

Dear Sierra,

You are the compass. You hand me round smooth stones as if they are precious jewels. Masterful collector. *Mama can you wash these?* I wash and dry. A weighted cache in my purse. The phone stays hidden. In-Suzuki-Roshi-slow-motion, we reach for Legos, sticks, sand, puzzle pieces. *I'm the baby bird and you are the Mama bird.* This love, impenetrable. Weekend ice cream party. Talk about Gerald and Piggie, best friends. Color outside lines. A temporary tattoo, indelible rainbow heart.

For Truong Tran

I Meant To Say

←—————————————————————————→

Butterfly bowl. Shadow child. Circles of paper and light. Grandness scoops fragility. Layers and layers of wings, laden with the body as a secret, sacred, feral container. Death by pin pricks, metamorphosis by cocoon bloom. The light strikes wings, shows every flaw, flesh and fabric. The rawness of innocence. The belief we can find our balance in mother-of-pearl inlays. A religion of the breath that no words speak. Wing markings that shift patterns with the color of a sigh. We are not alone, behind this glass. Needle holds firm, we are alive.

Courage Is

←——————————————————————→

Eye contact. To dive into the chasm. To seek. I have been sick for a few years now, but not the kind of sickness you suspect. I forget simple sounds like crows, mocking one another in the barely risen sun. Forgetting is silence. Forgetting is water, poured from a cliff. The tones of a singing Tibetan bowl. Forgotten. The sound of upstate New York snow piling high. Absence. A humble wooden desk at daybreak. Garbage cans dragged to the street. Yes. Yes to reflection. Yes to flight. Butterflies trace a pattern. Fly to the future in a metal pinion. Straight-no-chaser. One will arrive. One will depart.

Dear Winter,

The skies spattered with nickel-grey clouds. A lilt, warm breath. The sun's softness. Sudden droplets, mother nature's duties. Early mornings I sit in tranquility. The heart has no timeline. Crows in the yard again. Aerial gymnastics: treetop to roof, branch to grass, high wire to chimney. Congregation. They watch me. I reciprocate.

On March 8, 2014, Malaysia Air flight 370 vanished traveling from Kuala Lumpur to Beijing. The days that followed did not provide any conclusive findings of a crash nor wreckage.

News

←——————————————————————→

A plane disappears from the sky carrying two-hundred-thirty-nine people, an oil slick is all that skims the surface. Everyone holds their gasp. Where have they gone? Their spirits ride in the cumulus clouds. Coast along the silver horizon of the moon. Time passes, eyes mesmerized by lit up screens. A tennis ball volleyed between two sweaty men who resemble gazelles in the white desert dust. The agony of waiting. Friends and family are a trellis supporting a vine laden with fruit, bodies of whispers, minds of water. A muzak station pumps out The Cure, *I dreamt I was in love with you, strange as angels, just like a dream.* The mythos burns off like the Pacifica fog: all that remains is the gilded breath of the tides.

After Harryette Mullen

Dear N+7+8,

For no specific rebound I have become one of the clairvoyant's universes. No rare spectator, but one in rap of darling. No mythical announcement, but a common creel of urban lemon. No potent stanchion woven into poke and sorbet. Just the taut horny beautician you may observe, roaming at large in our hemorrhage. I'm known to advertisings in this circumscribed winch. Denatured physiognomies like to shoot me tipping the bouillon, snorting dustup, mousetrap on the wallpaper my horseshoe of empties that spilled the grasp's blot. My flight creations with itchy insomniacs. My heartthrob quotients as arteries. Tartar me for urban renegade. You can see that my hairpiece's stiffened and my skirt's thick, but the bravest champion can't dog my armor. How I know you so well. Why I know my own striker. Why, when I Charleston you with my rails, I will hold your gaze.

Riddle

←————————————————————→

I am the thing you cannot say. The momentum of speech stopped short. I am the gift inside the wrapping paper. I am the future. I am the turn of the page. The promise of a new text message. I am the ding ding ding. I am the signifier and signified. I am multiple targets, circular, never ending. I am the period. I am greater than Pi's 3.1 4 1 5 9 2 6 5 3 5 9. I am the soothsayer, fortune unrevealed. I am what comes next…

Dear Reader,

Finally they return. Their absence deafens. In the adjacent yard, they swoop and swallow. The orange geriatric tabby sits on the wooden fence. A crossbar juts out just enough for him to lie on. He watches my crows as if surveying his country. Chin on front paws. A leopard. Food dipped in water; they bring it to me. I am their avian goddess. In this hibernation, I need their boisterous reminder of life. The last vestiges removed, his shampoo and conditioner bottles discarded. These containers, time capsules. I am cycling in a hamster wheel. Not deflated, not a deadened thing. They resuscitate. I have a pulse.

Dear Reader,

To be obsessed with the sentence, the comma, the way it acts as a pause and a continuation, anticipation of the next thought, this nasty sentence structure, Virginia Woolf, guru of this linguistic religion. Lately I feel as if life is one long pause, one comma gouged deep into the page. A canyon of depth and width I cannot pass. How to continue? He lingers. An ellipsis, a comma, I desire finality. Finality. The red and green Christmas cheer, too much to bear. Sheer. Unseen. He's forgotten what it was like to love me. Moved on to a lowly simulacrum. An interloping lunatic obsessed with art stars, climbing a famed stairway. The dismissal of allegiance. The rest of the year resounds like a brass gong. Then, silence.

Three

You row forward looking back, and telling this history is part of helping people navigate toward the future. We need a litany, a rosary, a sutra, a mantra, a war chant for our victories. The past is set in daylight, and it can become a torch we can carry into the night that is the future.

— Rebecca Solnit, *Hope in Dark Times*

I have been trying, for some time now, to find dignity in my loneliness. I have been finding this hard to do.

— Maggie Nelson, "71," *Bluets*

Dear Loneliness,

I feel like a crow-black-wingéd thing. Today marks one year. I tally the days like evidence. I do not know why, or what spherical time patterns do to the façade. A geometry of the soul. I have settled into this idea of *without*. I wander in lacy seclusion with a certain softness and wonder. The crows are here again. Four atop a barren fig tree, two on the fence. They have their morning assemblage; I am certain they watch me through the thin pane of glass, pitch-dark plumage. Heated bickering, exodus. The geography they choose to encompass—perhaps they can illuminate.

Dear Love,

I hold on to the days. Passage of time is some unnamed currency. I will not be the solo survivor on an inflatable swan raft. I hang on, not for the reasons you suppose. It is to watch with every pore, every atom, the future come into focus. Take aloneness and shape it into epistolary convoys. The tangerine dahlia proves you still exist. I have trod the drought-ridden path of acceptance. What I want most: to feel it *is possible*, a sparkle coursing through my veins, balmy breath on the neck, hair erect, body shivers. My timekeeping predicts once the moon has orbited the earth twenty-four cycles, we will meet again. Until then, I am encircled by a thirty-foot electric fence. Until Stevie Wonder shows up in my dreams like a mercenary and confirms I am not all glass and alloy. He prods me to open one small window, to look at the legacy of longing.

Crave

⟵―――――――――――――――⟶

An atlas to discover and uncover. The light to show the exit path down the aisle. Vapors arise from a teacup and wisp like fallen dandelion wishes. The driving force is always love and forgiveness. I want ephemera from every place I visit — stones, postcards, leaves, sand. These relics ground and release. The ever-widening diaspora of memory. A *Wide Sargasso Sea*. The valley along the border of the Pacific Rim, out to boundless waters. A mermaid in the distance, flecks of sliver scales.

Drought

⟵─────────────────────────────⟶

That place without touch. To recollect the smell of a room thick with electric clouds. Sunday sweat under white flannel sheets. Sudden amnesia. Memory's chokehold. Thirst. I need replenishment. Water, electrolytes, endorphins. The atrophied muscle in dead center still pumps. How to mandate a honeyed survival. All is not barren. The white oleander subsists without.

You

←──────────────────────────────→

Are the lips that touch
the wine glass
and leave a perfect
shadow of lipstick. You are
the ice clinks in a
bartender's shaker,
poured with dexterity into
a delicious cocktail.
You are pine,
knotted and imperfect,
sanded down
to a smooth fine finish.
You are distressed Italian leather
of an expensive handbag
more beautiful as it ages.
You are the man in the sequined bowtie,
dressed to the nines
for no reason.
You are the woman
who breaks the glass ceiling
with her tits
in a push-up bra. You are
Brussels sprouts
sizzling in a cast iron skillet
devoured in five minutes flat.
You are the steps of solitude,
the comfort of silence.

Enough

←——————————————————————→

You wake in the morning with pillows, flannel sheets, the warm cocoon. You know the wisdom of early daylight, quiet sounds of the earth waking. You have weathered worse storms, death and illness have beaten down wood, but the house still stands. You rediscover the necessity of the pen, the blankness of the page, a blanket to guide you. You remember he is not a gladiator of love. You receive a love letter from a far-off voice. After ten years, this man still believes you were his greatest eclipse. Courage is enough.

Find an island; turn inward; discover your strength

— The RZA, *The Tao of Wu*

Dear Bravery,

You are groundless. A poker face in the DJ booth. Endurance, conditioning. The act of doing. Saying it. What's in your heart. *I think I love you a little bit.* I study crows as comfort. I head toward you, but I don't want anything from you. Put yourself in the space of the unknown. Water, sound, sand. Feel it change. Go forward without hesitation. Know there's fear. When the crows stop coming, where is the music? Put yourself on an island. Retreat. Talk about morning ritual, single parenthood. You help me see black history month through my whiteness. Bravery is the depth and width of connection.

Dear You,

And the days whoosh by like a bullet train. Threadbare by evening, you wrench yourself out of bed at daybreak. The tree outside is heavy with a black cluster of crows. Deafening bedlam. *Om Shanti Motherfuckers.* It is like relearning to walk, this isolation. You, who once had two additional hands, now heave the weight of two parents. The collage of life speeds past, blurs of turquoise, foliage, PSAs. Shake your head. Eyes open. Do this: *LOVE* your child. There *is* an infinite supply. Bury the past. Let it rot with the dirt in the yard. Fill your nest with shiny silver wrappers that astonish and mystify.

Strength

←——————————————————→

It comes from the squeeze. Pour a cup of green tea. *No response is a response.* Get dressed when you want to burrow. Cross the street, toward the blooms of a Magnolia. Do not look back. Show up for your students. Be honest. Notice the student in the back of the packed lecture hall, who you are pretty sure is homeless, the one who never removes his reflective Ray Bans. Do not lower your standards. We have a story to tell. Hold space. Resurrect the deflated. When all is said and divorced, slips of white paper notarized and FedExed, strength is the audacity to look at his face with kindness. Strength is soul. It comes from chaos. The lineage of women who have done it, alone.

To My Mother-In-Law On Blocking Her From Social Media

←——————————————————→

I had to disengage. The chimes of Facebook became a digital gang. Life too public. I could not. A shadow attached to self-preservation. Cracked steel girders of the Bay Bridge. The old bridge torn down piece by piece. We are decay. Alone in a colossal sea of six kinds of loneliness. I love you like my own mother. Wise. Intuitive. I know you carry this ache, a limestone around your neck. I reach for modest language. Garage decluttered, house empty. Stillness, an enclosure I cannot escape. Through the blinding heat, look for compassion and tenderness. Endings. Beginnings. No overtures of love nor regret. I cut ties with scissors. I mold and rewrap this burn. Ground Zero. A friend speaks the truth; we are no longer related. That truth circles, a Red-tailed Hawk in search of a field mouse. The mirror of loss. Unexpected harshness. No longer my mother, but I still feel your daughter. Long years of loving you. People are magnets, positive and negative. They ogle. Discordant rupture.

Hope is a waking dream.

— Aristotle

Dear Hope,

I dreamt you were an Adrienne Rich poem. I dreamt you were the softness of a woman's body, curves of words laid out like calligraphy of desire. I dreamt of a new lover coming over for dinner for the first time, fingers in a red bowl of spaghetti and later in my mouth. I dreamt of an entire weekend inside the sea's sway and froth. I dreamt you were a perfect poem, with all the hauntings of hurt, hope of arousal. I dreamt of writing one long sentence that summed up the pain and regret in the world and spat out tiny, dazzling, words stitched together as solace.

Dear Love,

Chaos subsides. Lilt of a voice. The skeletal tree laden with crows, beacons of darkness. They sit on emptiness with grandeur. Speak language of conflict. Broken wings. How to steal more time from the day. How to wake and dredge oneself out of the interior. Talk about flight through soul music. D'Angelo's third coming. Redemption. Black Messiah. *You've got to pray for redemption, lord, keep me away from temptation. Give me peace. Believe that love.*

For R.M.

Encounter

⟵─────────────────────⟶

Does it rest in the stretch of a six-foot-six smile? Fingers intertwined with another's? Found in the lover's whistle down the hotel corridor? Is it in the call of seagulls, spread of a pelican's wingspan, buoyancy of afterglow? You have folded into a gaze, alchemy, density of the first five minutes. Drizzle of a sweet peach. The low notes of Fela's saxophone. Delicate questions in an elevator up to the sixteenth floor. Breathless leopards, rushed speech. Listen. Think about him afterward and know — that man is authentic.

After Bhanu Kapil

Dear Love,

Endings are the coefficient of beginnings. I traveled to Scotland. Responses in English. Voices of women. Birth, ancestry, residence. Forty years in this body of woman, how she moves through the day. Inside her. I don't know. Throbbing. Plum blossoms. Honey. I write because I cannot paint. Drawing a bath. Voluptuous *oh*. How to tell time with my body. It is winter; I don't open the window. Counting my in-breaths and my out-breaths, per second, minute, then hour. Bird calls. The sky above New York is thick red. I wrote to you, but you did not reply. I am trying to keep my heart open. This is my one jumping life. Fresh brown eggs. It is difficult to write about love. Lapsang souchong. The tea tastes of bark and wood-smoke. Her body is not in one straight line. She will never tell him. Notes on being a nomad. There are no faces like yours in this country. The April morning you turned your face away from what you secretly loved, and why? Because we can't take it— in a whole form. Writing is dangerous. And now the cantata begins. Then a gobbling silence. The fuchsia spikes of closed eyelids, dismembered kisses, arbitrary thirsts. I don't want to collect our stories anymore. Maybe Moss Beach. Maybe Philadelphia. I loved him according to the law of 45's. Abrupt. I think of Rilke, that bright face, inches from ore. I said no. I said yes. Saying: I can't. Sometimes you have to choose who you are. The only woman. The word lover is the same as a neatly folded manuscript you don't look at for a year. I always thought I'd marry in red, or pink, or orange. A crow begins to sing to his crow-wife who lives on the other side of the city. Tonight she does not answer. It's true. I miss his letters arriving, holding them between my fingertips like talismans. Clairvoyance. The body does not breathe in time. I want to make the book of looking: everything that has happened, everything that will happen. Twenty-four shapes of longing. The moonlight turns into pure red sun, and then the clouds, and then the earth. History of an outstretched arm. A paring knife in her right fist. The golden light in the trees. The inner skin, inverted, with its texture of overripe persimmons. The fruit falling off the bone. Her body open to the air. Interiors. To honor ellipsis. Interrogations become abstract. His questions grow eyes. How to live without expectation. How to travel light. How to let the earth go. How skin can see. This uncommon California rain that's falling as I write, the rain that reminds me I am always facing the direction of water: its rapidly dissolving salt.

Desire

←——————————————————————→

I want the breeze to kiss the small of my back. To be serenaded by guitar along the stone border of my pulsing heart. Bring the colors of dawn so I know you are serious. Leave all things digital behind. I want quartz, jasmine filled with sincerity. Give me your weathered, wrinkled, calloused hands. Let me trace the valley of erosion. I want to smell your conviction through times of loneliness and winter. You know the company a cup of hot tea brings. Rings of a tree tell time. Emotional purgatory filled with ephemera. Photos and letters should be buried and burnt. I want a madrone. The migration of branches, gnarled, roots deep. To go without, yet able to live with a pulse, a prayer. I want to tell you my desires, but I haven't met them all yet. The fantasy of white sands, mouth full of pillows, lavender buds, the scent of fennel on an afternoon walk. I want a lover who knows the empty cat dish isn't all. To walk in the desert and see you as an oasis. Tumbleweeds. Lizards. Through the valley to the ocean. I ask the froth and foam to read my palms.

Negotiating a wilderness
we have yet to know
this is where time stops
and we have none to go

— Patti Smith, "Wilderness"

Dear You,

I resolve to jostle through the crystalline crevices of dreams, a fanatic who loosens the bridle with a pen and ink. I long to feel brush strokes slide along the curves of my hips like days of old. There is learning in longing. The melancholic temperature of teacups, the sturdy reality of no reply, the digitized. What is this longing and when will it subside, if ever? Is this not the human condition? I long for my youth, wandering the streets with eyes aplomb. What of these relics that I hold from another lifetime? To keep or to throw away like the Japanese tidying expert suggests? With each, I question. Talisman or decayed memory? The dust motes blanket the typewriter, the poem in the bottle, the brass candelabra. I circle back to the continent where we began our life, this time, alone.

I saw a crow building a nest, I was watching him very carefully, I was kind of stalking him and he was aware of it. And you know what they do when they become aware of someone stalking them when they build a nest, which is a very vulnerable place to be? They build a decoy nest. It's just for you.

— Tom Waits

Definition

←——————————————————————→

I am splintered wood falling from the fence. The onionskin pages in the dictionary. The pinecone dropped from tree to perimeter. An Aspen connected beneath the grove. I am onyx, slate, a pointed arrow. The Scottish barmaid delivering pints. A Puffin in craggy cliffs. The Isle of Arran. The church bell's chime. The center target, full of questions. The squiggle of a question mark. I am daybreak. The poet mourning a city gone digital. The ghost that haunts with letters resurrected. The hunted, a solitary magpie. Shaolin in seek of a Master. Winter's bitterness. An affair with the Thesaurus. The wingspan of a twelve-foot albatross. I am the sea. I hold boats up by their curves. A thick wooden trunk, circles inside signify age. I am devoid of expectation and full of nests.

Acknowledgements

Thanks to *Two Hawks Quarterly*, which will include "Dear Loneliness" in their Spring 2016 issue.

I'm ever grateful to the clan of family and friends who have kept me whole during the process of writing this book. You provided company, warm arms, an ear, a shoulder, spent holidays, birthdays, vacations and filled empty weekends with immeasurable love.

Thanks to the entire Keir clan: Mom, Dad, Colin, Melissa, Fancy Pants and Sierra. Your spirited support allowed this book to be written.

Jennifer Barone, connected by way of love, loss, poetry and an insatiable desire to learn what comes next (Kung Fu, booyacatcha). I hold so much admiration and gratitude to you, dear badass, who whipped these words into a gorgeously designed book.

Melissa Acedera, who got on a plane, who knows all my secrets and is the one I'll call if I need to move a dead body. Mac McIntosh and Reggie Sparks, I am grateful for your pillars of tender wisdom and ability to constantly reinvent and inspire. Eva Mosakowski, who provided a balance of gaiety and introspection, with the cosmos on speed dial. Kim and Keith Laidlaw, who took care of me during those dark nights of the soul that required a hug, a warm meal and some contraband whisky. Afi Ayanna, who will always help me face the truth with resolve and compassion. Sarah Cain, for reminding me to be kinder to myself every now and again. Lisa Guillot, for helping me see both sides and remember what it is to be human.

There are many others who have provided perspective and friendship while I was writing this book: Lisa Alden, Elisabeth Beaird, Lynn Belcher, Gary Bishop, The Briggs family, The Brogi clan, MK Chavez, Mathias Fain, The Gajda clan, Trey Gerfers,

Angela Hayward, Daniel Heffez, Matt Hessburg, Kathy Homan, Erin Kinsella, Kyle Knobel, Pauline Laidlaw, Denise LaCongo, Beth Lisick, Richard Loranger, Zanna McFerson, Rich Medina, Emily Mesko, Katie Mitchell, Tomas Moniz, Elizabeth Nails, Philip T Nails, Ploi Pirapokin Charity Read, The Reeves clan, Brion Nuda Rosch, Alena Rudolph, Jonathan Siegel, Charlie Villyard and Jason Williams.

The poetry Sensei who gave me a lighted path: Sharon Doubiago, Kim Addonizio, Neeli Cherkovski, and David Meltzer.

For my students, who taught me far more than I could ever imagine.

The stellar faculty at San Francisco State University, who provided thoughtful responses to my scribbles in various iterations: Truong Tran, Paul Hoover, Maxine Chernoff, Nona Caspers, Barbara Tomash and the late Stacy Doris.

To the WordParty poets and musicians, who bless the Bay Area with something sacred and pivotal in a city that increasingly devalues art. You keep the soul coursing through the veins of our streets.

Sincere thanks to Elise O'Keefe for her keen eye and willingness to proofread with sincerity and resolve.

Special thanks and eternal gratitude to the talented and wonderful Kelly Ording for allowing me to use her beautiful artwork throughout this book. kellyording.com

And finally, to my daughter, who shows me what it means to believe in the currency of kindness. I am forever bound by your spirit, laughter and love.

If I have inadvertently left anyone out, please forgive me. I'll write you a poem.

References

Addonizio, Kim. "Body and Soul." *What Is This Thing Called Love*. 95. New York: W.W. Norton & Company, 2004.

Chernoff, Maxine. *"Rune."* Here, 6. Denver: Counterpath, 2014.

Chin, Justin. "Imagining America." *Harmless Medicine*, 73. San Francisco: Manic D Press, 2001.

Cohen, Leonard. "Dance Me to the End of Love." *Various Positions*. New York: Colombia, 1985. LP.

Cure, The. "Just Like Heaven." *Kiss Me, Kiss Me, Kiss Me*. London: Fiction, 1987. LP.

D'Angelo and the Vanguard. "Prayer." *Black Messiah*. New York: RCA, 2014. LP.

Didion, Joan. *Blue Nights*, 4. New York: Vintage International, 2012.

Doubiago, Sharon. "The Geography of My Soul, 2." *Body & Soul*, 127. Mena: Cedar Hill Publications, 2000.

Haupt, Lyanda Lynn. Crow *Planet: Essential Wisdom from the Urban Wilderness*. New York: Little, Brown and Company, 2009.

Jong, Erica. "Testament (Or, Homage to Walt Whitman)." *Loveroot*, 3. New York: Holt, Rinehart and Winston, 1968.

Kapil Rider, Bhanu. *The Vertical Interrogation of Strangers*. Kelsey Street Press, 2009.

Nelson, Maggie. "71." *Bluets*, 28. Seattle: Wave Books, 2009.

Neruda, Pablo. "If You Forget Me." *The Captain's Verses*, translated by Donald D. Walsh, 77. New York: New Directions, 2004.

Pareles, Jon. "Q and A with Tom Waits." *The New York Times*, 2011.

Rich, Adrienne. "To The Days." *Dark Fields of the Republic*, 5. New York: W.W. Norton & Company, 1995.

RZA, The Tao of Wu, *The Tao of Wu*, 19. New York: Riverhead Books, 2009.

Shakespeare, William. "Sonnet 43." *Sonnets*, 43. New York: State Street Press, 2000.

Solnit, Rebecca. *Hope in Dark Times*. Chicago: Haymarket Books, 2016.

Smith, Patti. "Wilderness." *Auguries of Innocence*, 44. New York: Ecco, 2008.

Strayed, Cheryl. "Write Like a Motherfucker." Tiny Beautiful Things, *Advice on Love and Life from Dear Sugar,* 60. New York, Vintage Books, 2012.

Whitman, Walt. "Song of Myself." *Leaves of Grass*, 44. New York: Viking Penguin Inc., 1959.

About the Author

Ingrid Keir is a poet, performer and educator. She is co-founder of the WordParty, a long-running San Francisco poetry and jazz series. She has been a featured reader at diverse venues in the Bay Area including the DeYoung Museum, The Beat Museum, City Hall, Quiet Lightning as well as many others. Ingrid has lectured Creative Writing at San Francisco State University where she taught undergraduate poetry, fiction and playwriting while simultaneously engaging students with writers of the Bay Area. She also received both her M.F.A and B.A. degrees at San Francisco State University. She has written several chapbooks: *The Secrets of Like* (2004), *Toward the Light* (2007) and has been published in many literary journals including: *Two Hawks Quarterly, The Haight Ashbury Literary Journal, Sparkle and Blink* and *Out of Our*. Please see www.ingrid-keir.com for more info.

www.ingramcontent.com/pod-product-compliance
Lightning Source LLC
Chambersburg PA
CBHW030500010526
44118CB00011B/1021